curries

bay books

Contents

An Exotic Culinary Journey

Who can resist the heady aroma of spices, lazily wafting from a slowly simmering curry? Conjuring up images of exotic far-flung destinations, the ready availability of such a huge array of spices means that these days any of us can recreate an Indian or Thai feast in our own kitchens.

The word 'curry' comes from the East Indian word kari or karhi, meaning sauce, and traditionally refers to any spiced wet, or gravy-based, dish of Indian origin. However, 'curry' has been adopted around the world and now covers a multitude of recipes, with varying degrees of heat and spice, and served wet or dry. Indeed, contrary to popular belief, some curries have no heat or pungent flavours at all.

Many people think only of India whenever curry is mentioned, and indeed there are many recipes from Thailand, Sri Lanka, Malaysia, Vietnam and Jamaica to broaden your culinary horizons.

THE SPICE TRADE

Evidence of the use of spices dates back to the earliest known written records, belonging to the ancient Assyrians – sesame wine was drunk by the gods the night before they created the earth. There are also references to the use of spices in Egyptian hieroglyphs and even in the Bible – Joseph, of the coat of many colours, was sold to Egyptian spice traders by his brothers.

Spices were introduced to the West by Arab traders in about 2000 BC. They soon became extremely valuable and an important trade commodity, hence the commencement of the 'spice trade'. Indeed, much of the West's exploration of the world was driven by the desire to dominate the spice trade. Back then, spices were not only used for flavouring food and drink, but also preserving foods and masking the flavour of partially spoiled meats. Naturally, for some time, only the wealthy could afford spices and they continued to be a

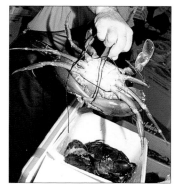

luxury, unobtainable to the poor man until the nineteenth century.

COOKING CURRIES

Luckily today we can all cook a curry anytime we feel like it and we are fortunate to have a multitude of fresh and exotic spices at our fingertips. Fresh spices are absolutely essential for achieving the correct flavour in your curries and should be purchased in small amounts, with leftovers stored in airtight containers in a cool, dark place so they do not go stale or rancid. If your spices are a little stale you can still use them but you may need to add a touch more than the recipe suggests to obtain the maximum flavour. Traditionally, authentic curries are made from scratch, which includes the toasting and grinding of all your spices. We have included instructions for this, however for the sake of convenience some recipes suggest using ready-ground spices.

While there is some work involved in making a good curry, one of the great things about them is that they can usually be made a day or two ahead. The flavour is often enhanced by leaving the curry, covered and refrigerated, for up to three days. The only exception is a seafood curry, which should be eaten the same day it is made.

Each curry in this book is given a heat rating, from one to three chillies, which is essential for the curry novice. As you become accustomed to a certain heat level you may wish to be a little adventurous and try something hotter and spicier.

Some curries contain coconut cream or milk, ghee, butter and cream, and are high in fat and therefore not suitable for those on a low-fat diet. However, if you can't resist, try using reduced-fat coconut milk. You can also replace full-fat cream with low-fat cream or yoghurt where necessary, however be aware that the curry will not have the same flavour or texture.

Glossary

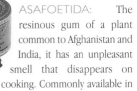

ASAFOETIDA: The resinous gum of a plant common to Afghanistan and India, it has an unpleasant smell that disappears on cooking. Commonly available in powdered form, it is used as a seasoning, or as a substitute for onion and garlic.

BASMATI RICE: Aromatic long narrow- grained rice. The grains remain firm and separate when cooked. Used for biryani and pilau dishes.

BESAN (CHICKPEA FLOUR): A pale yellow flour made from ground chickpeas and used in Indian cuisine, giving a unique texture. Often used as a thickener in sauces and batters.

BLACK, BROWN, YELLOW AND WHITE MUSTARD SEEDS: A common ingredient in many curries, mustard seeds are fried before grinding to release essential oils and increase their flavour. Black and brown mustard seeds are the smallest and hottest, whereas yellow and white mustard seeds are larger and milder.

CANDLENUTS: A hard, pale nut about 20 mm in diameter. They must be cooked as they are mildly toxic when raw. The nut is ground, grated or pounded before use as a thickening agent in dishes from Thailand, Indonesia and Malaysia. Store in the refrigerator, or better still, the freezer, as their high oil content means they become rancid quite quickly.

CARDAMOM: A very aromatic spice of Indian origin, available as whole pods, whole seeds or ground. The pale green oval pods, each up to 1.5 cm long, are tightly packed with spicy, sweet and pungent brown or black seeds. Lightly bruise the pods before adding to the dish. Crush the pods to extract the seeds, if required.

CASSIA BARK: This spice comes from the inner bark of a tropical evergreen tree. It closely resembles cinnamon, and is often used either in conjunction with, or in place of, it.

COCONUT MILK AND CREAM: Both are extracted from the grated flesh of mature coconuts. The cream is a richer, thicker first pressing and the milk the second or third pressing. Don't shake the coconut cream can as some recipes require the thick cream on the top.

CORIANDER: Also known as cilantro, coriander is the most common herb in Thai cooking. It is an aromatic, green leafy herb used to flavour and garnish. The whole plant is used – roots, stems and leaves. The seeds can be roasted whole and are often ground.

CUMIN: One of the important flavours in curry powders and pastes, this nutty flavoured aromatic spice is available both in seeds and ground.

CURRY LEAVES: Used in Asian cooking, especially Sri Lankan and East Indian curries. They are small, pointed leaves with a natural spicy, toasty curry flavour. Remove before serving.

DRIED SHRIMP: Tiny, salted shrimp that have been dried in the sun. Used for added flavour, especially in sauces. Also available ground to a powder. Take care when using the powder as it can be intensely flavoured and salty. They are often roasted before use.

FENNEL SEEDS: These yellow–brown aromatic seeds taste of aniseed and are used to flavour many Indian dishes.

FENUGREEK: Aromatic seeds which are dry-fried and ground, then added to curry pastes or used in Indian dishes. They are slightly sweet, but use sparingly as the flavour can be bitter.

FISH SAUCE: A brown, salty sauce with a characteristic 'fishy' smell, it is an important ingredient in Thai and Vietnamese cookery. It is made from small fish that have been fermented in the sun for a long time.

GALANGAL: Related to ginger, with a peppery flavour and pinkish colour. Available in dried form as Laos.

GARAM MASALA: A blend of spices usually consisting of cinnamon, coriander, cumin, black pepper, cloves, fennel, cardamom, nutmeg and mace. It can be bought ready-made, but is best freshly made. It is usually added towards the end of cooking.

GHEE: Clarified, unsalted butter used in Indian cooking because it reaches high temperatures before it smokes, unlike some other oils and fats.

JAPANESE CURRY: Comes in a solid block or in powder form and is available in Asian supermarkets. Various degrees of heat are available.

JASMINE RICE: A long-grain, fragrant white rice used throughout South-East Asia. Usually steamed or cooked using the absorption method, and then served as an accompaniment.

KAFFIR LIME AND LEAVES: A knobbly, dark-skinned lime with a very strong fragrance and flavour. The leaves have a very pungent perfume. They are thick and must be thinly sliced for use in curry pastes and salads or used whole in curries. The grated rind is also used in curries.

KECAP MANIS: A thick, sweet soy sauce, widely used in Indonesia and Malaysia as a seasoning or condiment.

LEMON GRASS: An aromatic, thick-stemmed herb often used in Thai cooking. Remove the tough, outer stem and thinly slice or chop. The whole stem may be used and removed before serving, however, more commonly, only the white part is used. Dried lemon grass is available but must be reconstituted and is inferior in flavour.

PALM SUGAR: Sold in blocks or jars and ranges in colour from pale gold to dark brown. It is a rich aromatic sugar extracted from various palms. Soft brown sugar can be substituted.

PANDAN LEAF: Used in both sweet and savoury dishes, this long, mildly aromatic leaf is often used to enclose small parcels of food before cooking or to lend a subtle but distinctive flavour to rice dishes. Available fresh and frozen in Asian food stores.

RED ASIAN SHALLOTS: Small reddish/purple onions, these grow in bulbs and are sold in segments that look like large cloves of garlic. They have a concentrated flavour and are easy to slice and grind. If necessary, use red onions as a substitute – one small red onion to 3–4 Asian shallot segments.

SAFFRON THREADS: These reddish-orange threads are the stigmas of a crocus flower. Saffron is the most expensive spice in the world, but only a small amount is needed to give a vivid colour and subtle flavour. The strands are generally infused in a little hot water before using.

SHRIMP PASTE: A pungent brown paste made by salting, fermenting and grinding shrimp. Use sparingly to flavour curry pastes or sauces. It is available in a block or thick paste.

STAR ANISE: The dried, star-shaped seed pod of a tree native to China. Adds a distinctive aniseed taste to long-simmered meat and poultry dishes and is one of the components of five spice powder.

TAMARIND: Tamarind has a fruity, tart flavour, and is a large, brown bean-like pod. It is available as a dried shelled fruit, a block of compressed pulp or as a purée or concentrate.

THAI OR HOLY BASIL: A member of the basil family with smaller, darker leaves than regular basil. It also has a stronger aniseed and clove flavour and aroma. Leaves are added whole or chopped to curries and stir-fries.

TURMERIC: Available fresh and dried, turmeric is best known in its powdered form and is often used to colour food deep yellow or orange. It has a bitter, pungent flavour. Care should be taken when using fresh turmeric as it will stain your hands and clothes.

VIETNAMESE MINT: Also called laksa leaf and Cambodian mint, this trailing herb with narrow, pointed, pungent-tasting leaves does not belong to the mint family, despite its common name. Its flavour resembles coriander, but slightly sharper, and it is eaten raw in salads.

Curry pastes

MADRAS CURRY PASTE

Preparation time: 5 minutes
Total cooking time: Nil
Makes ½ cup

2½ tablespoons coriander seeds,
  dry-roasted and ground
1 tablespoon cumin seeds, dry-roasted
  and ground
1 teaspoon brown mustard seeds
½ teaspoon cracked black peppercorns
1 teaspoon chilli powder
1 teaspoon ground turmeric
2 cloves garlic, crushed
2 teaspoons grated fresh ginger
3–4 tablespoons white vinegar

1 Place the ground coriander, ground cumin, mustard seeds, cracked black peppercorns, chilli powder, ground turmeric, garlic, ginger and 1 teaspoon salt in a small bowl, and mix together well. Add the vinegar and mix to a smooth paste. Store in a clean airtight container jar in the refrigerator for up to a month.

GENERAL PURPOSE INDIAN CURRY POWDER

Preparation time: 5 minutes
Total cooking time: 3 minutes
Makes ⅓ cup

2 teaspoons cumin seeds
2 teaspoons coriander seeds
2 teaspoons fenugreek seeds
1 teaspoon yellow mustard seeds
1 teaspoon black peppercorns
1 teaspoon whole cloves
1 teaspoon chilli powder
2 teaspoons ground turmeric
½ teaspoon ground cinnamon
½ teaspoon ground cardamom

1 Dry-fry the whole spices separately in a small frying pan over medium heat for 2–3 minutes, or until fragrant. Place in a spice grinder, mortar and pestle or small food processor with a fine blade, and grind to a fine powder.
2 Place in a small bowl with the pre-ground spices and mix together well. Store in an airtight container in a cool, dark place.

SRI LANKAN CURRY POWDER

Preparation time: 5 minutes
Total cooking time: 20 minutes
Makes ⅓ cup

3 tablespoons coriander seeds
1½ tablespoons cumin seeds
1 teaspoon fennel seeds
¼ teaspoon fenugreek seeds
2 cm cinnamon stick
6 cloves
¼ teaspoon cardamom seeds
2 teaspoons dried curry leaves
2 small dried red chillies

1 Dry-fry the coriander, cumin, fennel and fenugreek seeds separately over low heat until fragrant. It is important to do this separately, as all spices brown at different rates. Make sure the spices are well browned, not burnt.
2 Place the browned seeds in a food processor, blender or mortar and pestle, add the remaining ingredients and process or grind to a powder. Store in an airtight container in a cool, dry place.

VINDALOO PASTE

Preparation time: 10 minutes
Total cooking time: Nil
Makes ½ cup

2 tablespoons grated fresh ginger
4 cloves garlic, chopped
4 red chillies, chopped
2 teaspoons ground turmeric
2 teaspoons ground cardamom
4 whole cloves
6 peppercorns
1 teaspoon ground cinnamon
1 tablespoon ground coriander
1 tablespoon cumin seeds
½ cup (125 ml) cider vinegar

1 Place all the ingredients in a food processor and process for 20 seconds, or until well combined and smooth. Refrigerate for up to a month.

GARAM MASALA

Preparation time: 7 minutes
Total cooking time: 3 minutes
Makes ½ cup

2 tablespoons coriander seeds
1½ tablespoons cardamom pods
1 tablespoon cumin seeds
2 teaspoons whole black peppercorns
1 teaspoon whole cloves
3 cinnamon sticks
1 nutmeg, grated

1 Dry-fry all the ingredients, except the nutmeg, separately in a frying pan over medium heat for 2–3 minutes, or until fragrant.
2 Remove the cardamom pods, crush with the handle of a heavy knife and remove the seeds. Discard the pods.
3 Place the fried spices, cardamom seeds and nutmeg in a food processor, blender or mortar and pestle, and process or grind to a powder. Store in an airtight container in a cool, dark place.

GREEN CURRY PASTE

Preparation time: 30 minutes
Total cooking time: 10 minutes
Makes 1 cup

1 teaspoon white peppercorns
1 teaspoon cumin seeds
2 tablespoons coriander seeds
2 teaspoons shrimp paste (wrapped in foil)
1 teaspoon sea salt
4 stems lemon grass, white part only, finely chopped
2 teaspoons chopped fresh galangal
2 teaspoons finely shredded kaffir lime leaves
1 tablespoon chopped fresh coriander root
5 red Asian shallots, chopped
10 cloves garlic, chopped
16 large green chillies, seeded and chopped

1 Preheat the oven to moderate 180°C (350°F/Gas 4). Place the peppercorns, cumin and coriander seeds, and shrimp paste in a baking dish, and bake for 5–10 minutes, or until fragrant. Remove the foil.
2 Place all the ingredients in a food processor or mortar and pestle, and process or grind to a smooth paste. Store in an airtight container in the refrigerator for up to a month.

RED CURRY PASTE

Preparation time: 20 minutes + soaking
Total cooking time: 10 minutes
Makes 1 cup

15 dried large red chillies
1 teaspoon white peppercorns
2 teaspoons coriander seeds
1 teaspoon cumin seeds
2 teaspoons shrimp paste (wrapped in foil)
5 red Asian shallots, chopped
10 cloves garlic
2 stems lemon grass, white part only, finely sliced
1 tablespoon chopped fresh galangal
2 tablespoons chopped fresh coriander root
1 teaspoon finely grated kaffir lime rind

1 Preheat the oven to moderate 180°C (350°F/Gas 4). Soak the chillies in boiling water for 10 minutes. Remove the seeds and roughly chop the flesh.
2 Place the spices and shrimp paste in a baking dish, place in the oven and bake for 5–10 minutes, or until fragrant. Remove the foil.
3 Place all the ingredients in a food processor or mortar and pestle, and process or grind to a smooth paste. Store in an airtight container in the refrigerator for up to a month.

MUSAMAN CURRY PASTE

Preparation time: 20 minutes + soaking
Total cooking time: 5 minutes
Makes ½ cup

10 dried large red chillies
3 cardamom pods
1 teaspoon cumin seeds
1 tablespoon coriander seeds
1 teaspoon shrimp paste (wrapped in foil)
5 red Asian shallots, chopped
¼ teaspoon black peppercorns

1 stem lemon grass, white part only, finely chopped
1 tablespoon chopped fresh galangal
10 cloves garlic, chopped
¼ teaspoon ground cinnamon
½ teaspoon ground nutmeg
¼ teaspoon ground cloves

1 Preheat the oven to moderate 180°C (350°F/Gas 4). Soak the chillies in boiling water for 10 minutes, drain, remove the seeds and roughly chop.
2 Place the whole spices, shrimp paste, shallots, lemon grass, galangal and garlic in a baking dish, and bake for 5 minutes, or until fragrant. Remove the foil.
3 Place the chilli, roasted ingredients and ground spices in a food processor, mortar and pestle or spice grinder, and process or grind to a smooth paste. If the mixture is too dry add a little vinegar to moisten it. Store in an airtight container in the refrigerator for up to a month.

Madkasi Kari (Madras Beef Curry)

PREPARATION TIME: 20 minutes
TOTAL COOKING TIME: 1 hour 45 minutes
SERVES 4

1 tablespoon oil or ghee
1 onion, chopped
3–4 tablespoons Madras curry paste
1 kg skirt or chuck steak, trimmed and cut
 into 2.5 cm cubes
¼ cup (60 g) tomato paste
1 cup (250 ml) beef stock

1 Heat the oil in a large frying pan, add the onion and cook over medium heat for 10 minutes, or until browned. Add the curry paste and stir for 1 minute, or until fragrant. Then add the meat and cook, stirring, until coated with the curry paste. Stir in the tomato paste and stock. Reduce the heat and simmer, covered, for 1 hour 15 minutes, and then uncovered for 15 minutes, or until the meat is tender.

Trim the meat of any excess fat or sinew and cut into cubes.

Cook the onion in a large frying pan until browned.

Add the meat to the pan and stir to coat in the curry paste.

Gosht Kari (Basic Lamb Curry)

PREPARATION TIME: 40 minutes
TOTAL COOKING TIME: 2 hours 10 minutes
SERVES 6

1.5 kg lamb, cut into 3 cm cubes
⅓ cup (80 ml) oil
2 large onions, finely chopped
4–6 cloves garlic, chopped
1 tablespoon grated fresh ginger
2 small red chillies, seeded and chopped
1 tablespoon ground cumin
1 tablespoon ground coriander
2 teaspoons ground turmeric
½ teaspoon chilli powder
2 x 400 g cans crushed tomatoes
1 tablespoon tomato paste
4 tablespoons chopped fresh coriander

1 Heat 1 tablespoon of the oil in a large saucepan, add a third of the lamb and cook over high heat for 4 minutes, or until browned. Remove. Repeat twice more with the remaining lamb and 2 more tablespoons oil. Remove all the lamb from the pan.

2 Heat the remaining oil in the saucepan. Add the onion and cook over medium heat, stirring frequently, for 10 minutes, or until golden. Add the garlic, ginger and chilli, and cook for 2 minutes, then add the ground spices and cook, stirring, for a further 3 minutes, or until fragrant.

3 Add the tomato, tomato paste, the lamb and 1 teaspoon salt. Mix thoroughly, then reduce the heat and simmer, covered, for 1½ hours, or until the meat is tender. Stir occasionally.

4 Uncover, increase the heat and cook for 10 minutes to allow the sauce to reduce and thicken. Garnish with the coriander and serve with rice or boiled potatoes.

Brown the lamb in a large saucepan in three batches.

Cook onion, stirring frequently, until softened and golden.

Ooroomas Badun (Sri Lankan Fried Pork Curry)

PREPARATION TIME: 45 minutes
TOTAL COOKING TIME: 1 hour 40 minutes
SERVES 6

1.25 kg boned pork shoulder, cut into 3 cm
  cubes
⅓ cup (80 ml) oil
1 large red onion, finely chopped
3–4 cloves garlic, crushed
1 tablespoon grated fresh ginger
10 curry leaves
½ teaspoon fenugreek seeds
½ teaspoon chilli powder
6 cardamom pods, bruised
2 tablespoons Sri Lankan curry powder
1 tablespoon white vinegar
⅓ cup (105 g) tamarind concentrate
270 ml coconut cream

1 Heat half the oil in a large saucepan over high heat, add the meat and cook in batches for 6 minutes, or until well browned. Remove from the pan.

2 Heat the remaining oil, add the onion and cook over medium heat for 5 minutes, or until lightly browned. Add the garlic and ginger, and cook for 2 minutes. Stir in the curry leaves, spices and curry powder, and cook for 2 minutes, or until fragrant. Stir in the vinegar and 1 teaspoon salt.

3 Return the meat to the pan, add the tamarind and 1¼ cups (315 ml) water and simmer, covered, for 50 minutes, or until the meat is tender. Stir occasionally. Stir in the coconut cream and simmer, uncovered, for 15 minutes, or until the sauce has reduced and thickened a little. Serve with rice.

Cook the meat in batches for 6 minutes, or until well browned.

Cook the onion over medium heat until lightly browned.

Simmer, uncovered, until the sauce has reduced and thickened.

19

Katsu Kare (Japanese Pork Schnitzel Curry)

PREPARATION TIME: 25 minutes
TOTAL COOKING TIME: 30 minutes
SERVES 4

1 tablespoon oil
1 onion, cut into thin wedges
2 large carrots, cut into 2 cm cubes
1 large potato, cut into 2 cm cubes
60 g Japanese curry paste block, broken
   into small pieces
flour, for coating
4 x 120 g pork schnitzels, pounded to 4 mm
   thickness
2 eggs, lightly beaten
150 g Japanese breadcrumbs (panko)
oil, for deep-frying
pickled ginger, pickled daikon, umeboshi
   (baby pickled plums), crisp fried onions, to
   garnish

1 Heat the oil in a saucepan, add the onion, carrot and potato, and cook over medium heat for 10 minutes, or until starting to brown. Add 2 cups (500 ml) water and the curry paste, and stir until the curry paste dissolves and the sauce becomes a smooth consistency. Reduce the heat and simmer for 10 minutes, or until the vegetables are cooked through. Season.

2 Season the flour well with salt and pepper. Dip each schnitzel into the flour, shake off any excess and dip into the beaten egg, allowing any excess to drip off. Coat with the Japanese breadcrumbs by pressing each side of the schnitzel firmly into the crumbs on a plate.

3 Fill a deep heavy-based saucepan one-third full of oil and heat to 180°C (350°F), or until a cube of bread dropped into the oil browns in 15 seconds. Cook the schnitzels, one at a time, turning once or twice, for 5 minutes, or until golden brown all over and cooked through. Drain on crumpled paper towels.

4 Slice each schnitzel into 5–6 pieces and arrange, keeping the original shape, over cooked rice. Ladle the curry sauce over the schnitzels. Garnish with fried onions and serve with the pickles on the side.

Cook the onion, carrot and potato until starting to brown.

Coat the schnitzels in flour, egg and then Japanese breadcrumbs.

Shikar Dopiaza (Pork and Onion Stew)

PREPARATION TIME: 20 minutes

TOTAL COOKING TIME: 1 hour 45 minutes

SERVES 4–6

1 kg onions

5 cloves garlic

1 tablespoon grated fresh ginger

2 small red chillies, chopped

1 teaspoon paprika

4 tablespoons chopped fresh coriander
  leaves

2 tablespoons ground coriander

2 teaspoons nigella seeds

⅓ cup (90 g) plain yoghurt

⅓ cup (80 g) ghee or oil

1 kg diced pork

6 cardamom pods, lightly crushed

1 teaspoon garam masala

1 Slice half the onions and set aside. Roughly chop the remaining onions.

2 Place the chopped onion, garlic, ginger, chilli, paprika, fresh and ground coriander, nigella seeds and yoghurt in a food processor, and process to a smooth paste.

3 Heat the ghee in a large saucepan, add the sliced onion and cook over medium heat for 10 minutes, or until golden brown. Remove from the pan with a slotted spoon and drain on crumpled paper towels.

4 Add the diced pork to the pan in batches and cook over high heat for 3–5 minutes, or until browned. Remove from the pan and cover loosely with foil to keep warm.

5 Add spice paste to the pan and cook for 5 minutes, or until the ghee starts to separate from the onion. Reduce the heat to low, return the meat to the pan, add the cardamom and cook, covered, for 1 hour, or until the meat is tender.

6 Add the fried onion and garam masala to the pan, and cook for another 15 minutes. Serve with rice and naan bread.

Mix herbs and spices, add yoghurt and process to a smooth paste.

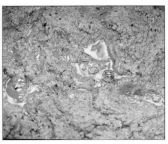

Cook spice paste until the ghee starts to separate from the onion.

Gaeng Phed Nuek Makua (Thai Red Beef Curry with Thai Eggplant)

PREPARATION TIME: 40 minutes
TOTAL COOKING TIME: 1 hour 30 minutes
SERVES 4

1 cup (250 ml) coconut cream (do not shake the can)
2 tablespoons red curry paste
500 g round or topside steak, cut into strips
2 tablespoons fish sauce
1 tablespoon palm sugar
5 kaffir lime leaves, halved
2 cups (500 ml) coconut milk
8 Thai eggplants, halved
2 tablespoons finely shredded fresh Thai basil leaves

1 Place the thick coconut cream from the top of the can in a wok and bring to the boil. Boil for 10 minutes, or until the oil starts to separate. Add the curry paste and simmer, stirring to prevent it sticking to the bottom, for 5 minutes, or until fragrant.

2 Add the meat and cook, stirring, for 3–5 minutes, or until it changes colour. Add the fish sauce, palm sugar, lime leaves, coconut milk and remaining coconut cream, and simmer for 1 hour, or until the meat is tender and the sauce slightly thickened.

3 Add the eggplant and cook for 10 minutes, or until tender. If the sauce is too thick, add a little water. Stir in half the basil leaves. Garnish with the remaining basil leaves and serve with rice.

Using a sharp knife, cut the meat across the grain into thin strips.

Boil the thick coconut cream until the oil separates from the cream.

Add the meat to the wok and cook until it changes colour.

25

Lamb Neck Curry

PREPARATION TIME: 30 minutes
TOTAL COOKING TIME: 1 hour 35 minutes
SERVES 4–6

1 tablespoon oil
8 best lamb neck chops
2 onions, sliced
3 cloves garlic, finely chopped
2 teaspoons finely chopped fresh ginger
1 small green chilli, seeded and finely
  chopped
½ teaspoon ground cumin
1 teaspoon ground fennel
1½ teaspoons ground turmeric
1½ teaspoons chilli powder
2 teaspoons garam masala
1 star anise
1 cinnamon stick
5 curry leaves
2 bay leaves
2 cups (500 ml) beef stock
8 tomatoes, skinned and cut into quarters

1 Heat the oil in a large frying pan, add the lamb and cook in batches for 5–8 minutes, or until browned. Place in a large saucepan.

2 Add the onion to the frying pan and cook, stirring frequently, for 5 minutes, or until soft and browned. Stir in the garlic, ginger and green chilli and cook for 1 minute. Then stir in the cumin, fennel, turmeric, chilli powder, garam masala, star anise, cinnamon stick, curry leaves and bay leaves, and cook, stirring to prevent sticking, for a further 1 minute.

3 Add 2 tablespoons cold water to the frying pan, mix well, and then add the beef stock. Bring to the boil, then pour over the lamb. Stir in the tomato, reduce the heat and simmer, covered, for 1 hour 15 minutes. Serve with jasmine rice tossed with coriander.

Cook the lamb neck chops in batches until browned.

Stir the spices to prevent them sticking to the base of the pan.

27

Saag Gosht
(Lamb and Spinach Curry)

PREPARATION TIME: 30 minutes
TOTAL COOKING TIME: 2 hours 20 minutes
SERVES 6

1 kg English spinach
½ cup (125 ml) oil
1.5 kg lamb, cut into 3 cm cubes
2 red onions, finely chopped
6 cloves garlic, crushed
1½ tablespoons grated fresh ginger
2 bay leaves
2 tablespoons ground coriander
1 tablespoon ground cumin
1 teaspoon ground turmeric
2 large vine-ripened tomatoes, peeled,
  seeded and chopped
2–3 small green chillies, seeded and finely
  chopped
100 g plain thick yoghurt
1 cinnamon stick
2 teaspoons garam masala

1 Preheat oven to warm 170°C (325°F/Gas 3). Trim spinach and quickly blanch in simmering water. Drain, cool slightly and squeeze to remove excess moisture, then place in a food processor and process until smooth.

2 Heat half the oil in a large saucepan. Add lamb pieces in 3–4 batches and cook over high heat for 4–5 minutes, or until browned. Remove from pan.

3 Heat remaining oil in the saucepan. Add the onion and cook, stirring frequently, for 10 minutes, or until golden brown but not burnt. Add the garlic, ginger and bay leaves, and cook, stirring, for 3 more minutes.

4 Add the spices and cook, stirring, for 2 minutes, or until fragrant. Add the tomato and chilli, and stir over low heat for 5 minutes, or until the tomato is thick and pulpy. Remove from the heat and cool for 5 minutes. Transfer to a 4 litre oven-proof casserole dish and stir in the yoghurt.

5 Return the meat to the dish and add cinnamon stick and 1 teaspoon salt. Bake, covered, for 1 hour and then uncovered for a further 15 minutes. Stir in the spinach and garam masala, and cook, stirring occasionally, for 15 minutes, or until the meat is tender. Remove the bay leaves and cinnamon stick, and serve with rice or pilaf.

Process the spinach in a food processor until smooth.

Stir over low heat until the tomato is thick and pulpy.

Curried Beef Sausages

PREPARATION TIME: 20 minutes
TOTAL COOKING TIME: 45 minutes
SERVES 6–8

1 onion, chopped
2 cloves garlic
1 teaspoon chopped fresh ginger
2 teaspoons curry powder
1 teaspoon chilli powder
1½ teaspoons paprika
3 teaspoons poppy seeds
2 tablespoons oil
1.25 kg medium-size good-quality beef
  sausages
6 tomatoes, skinned, quartered and seeded
2 tablespoons mango chutney
1⅔ cups (420 ml) coconut milk

1 Place the onion, garlic, ginger, curry powder, chilli powder, paprika and poppy seeds in a food processor, and process until smooth.

2 Heat 1 tablespoon of the oil in a large frying pan, add sausages in batches and cook for 6–8 minutes, or until browned on all sides. Remove and carefully wipe out the pan with paper towels. Leave the sausages to cool and slice into 1 cm thick slices.

3 Heat the remaining oil in the pan, add the spice paste and cook, stirring, for 2 minutes, or until fragrant. Mix in the tomato, mango chutney, coconut milk and sausages, and simmer, covered, for 20 minutes, stirring occasionally.

Process paste ingredients in a food processor until smooth.

Cook sausages in a large frying pan until browned on all sides.

Wipe out the pan with paper towels to remove any excess oil.

Shikar Vindaloo (Fiery Goan Pork Curry)

PREPARATION TIME: 20 minutes
TOTAL COOKING TIME: 2 hours
SERVES 4

1 kg pork fillets
¼ cup (60 ml) oil
2 onions, finely chopped
4 cloves garlic, finely chopped
1 tablespoon finely chopped fresh ginger
1 tablespoon garam masala
2 teaspoons brown mustard seeds
4 tablespoons vindaloo paste

1 Trim the pork of any excess fat and sinew and cut into bite-size pieces.

2 Heat the oil in a saucepan, add the meat in small batches and cook over medium heat for 5–7 minutes, or until browned. Remove from the pan.

3 Add the onion, garlic, ginger, garam masala and mustard seeds to the pan, and cook, stirring, for 5 minutes, or until the onion is soft.

4 Return all the meat to the pan, add the vindaloo paste and cook, stirring, for 2 minutes. Add 2½ cups (625 ml) water and bring to the boil. Reduce the heat and simmer, covered, for 1 hour 30 minutes, or until the meat is tender. Serve with boiled rice and pappadums.

Trim the pork of any excess fat or sinew and cut into cubes.

Cook the pork in small batches over medium heat until browned.

Add the vindaloo paste and cook until the meat is tender.

Keema Curry (Minced Beef and Pea Curry)

PREPARATION TIME: 15 minutes
TOTAL COOKING TIME: 40 minutes
SERVES 6

2 tablespoons oil
2 onions, chopped
1 clove garlic, finely chopped
1 tablespoon finely chopped fresh ginger
3 large green chillies, seeded and finely
  chopped
1½ tablespoons ground coriander
1 tablespoon ground cumin
2 teaspoons ground turmeric
750 g potatoes, cut into 1.5 cm cubes
1.5 kg minced beef
225 g frozen peas
⅔ cup (170 ml) coconut cream
1 tablespoon fresh coriander leaves,
  chopped

1 Heat the oil in a large saucepan, add the onion and cook, stirring frequently, for 5 minutes, or until lightly golden. Add the garlic, ginger and chilli, and cook for 1 minute, then add the coriander, cumin and turmeric and cook for a further 1 minute.

2 Add the potato and ½ cup (125 ml) water to the pan, and combine well. Cook, covered, over medium heat for 15 minutes. Add the beef and cook, uncovered, stirring frequently, over high heat, for 4–5 minutes, or until the mince is lightly browned. Break up any lumps with the back of a spoon. Stir in the peas and coconut cream.

3 Bring to the boil and cook, stirring occasionally, for 10 minutes, or until the curry is almost dry and the peas are cooked through. Season with salt and garnish with the coriander leaves. Serve with naan or pita bread.

Cook onion in a large saucepan for 5 minutes, until golden.

Break up any lumps in the mince with the back of a spoon.

Bring to the boil and cook, stirring, until the curry is almost dry.

34

Rogan Josh (Lamb in Spices and Yoghurt)

PREPARATION TIME: 25 minutes
TOTAL COOKING TIME: 1 hour 40 minutes
SERVES 4–6

1 kg boned leg of lamb
1 tablespoon ghee or oil
2 onions, chopped
½ cup (125 g) plain yoghurt
1 teaspoon chilli powder
1 tablespoon ground coriander
2 teaspoons ground cumin
1 teaspoon ground cardamom
½ teaspoon ground cloves
1 teaspoon ground turmeric
3 cloves garlic, crushed
1 tablespoon grated fresh ginger
400 g can chopped tomatoes
¼ cup (30 g) slivered almonds
1 teaspoon garam masala
chopped fresh coriander leaves, to garnish

1 Trim the lamb of any excess fat or sinew and cut into 2.5 cm cubes.

2 Heat ghee in a large saucepan, add onion and cook, stirring, for 5 minutes, or until soft. Stir in yoghurt, chilli powder, coriander, cumin, cardamom, cloves, turmeric, garlic and ginger. Add tomato and 1 teaspoon salt, and simmer for 5 minutes.

3 Add the lamb and stir until coated. Cover and cook over low heat, stirring occasionally, for 1–1½ hours, or until the lamb is tender. Uncover and simmer until the liquid thickens.

4 Meanwhile, toast the almonds in a dry frying pan over medium heat for 3–4 minutes, shaking the pan gently, until the nuts are golden brown. Remove from the pan at once to prevent them burning.

5 Add the garam masala to the curry and mix through well. Sprinkle the slivered almonds and coriander leaves over the top and serve.

Cook the onion in the ghee for 5 minutes, or until soft.

Remove the lid and simmer until the liquid thickens.

Toast the almonds in a dry frying pan until golden brown.

Murgh Kofta Shahi Korma (Chicken Meatballs with a Creamy Sauce)

PREPARATION TIME: 40 minutes
TOTAL COOKING TIME: 40 minutes
SERVES 4

Koftas
2 tablespoons oil
1 onion, finely chopped
1 clove garlic, crushed
1 teaspoon finely chopped fresh ginger
1 teaspoon ground cumin
1 teaspoon garam masala
½ teaspoon ground turmeric
650 g chicken thigh fillets, trimmed
2 tablespoons chopped fresh coriander

1 onion, roughly chopped
20 g ghee
2 cloves garlic, crushed
2 teaspoons garam masala
½ teaspoon ground turmeric
165 ml coconut milk
⅓ cup (90 g) plain yoghurt
½ cup (125 ml) cream
¼ cup (45 g) ground almonds
2 tablespoons chopped fresh coriander

Cook onion, garlic, ginger, cumin, garam masala and turmeric.

Process the chicken in batches until just chopped.

Shape the chicken mixture into even-size balls.

1 To make the koftas, heat half the oil in a frying pan, add the onion, garlic, ginger, ground cumin, garam masala and ground turmeric, and cook, stirring, for 4–6 minutes, or until the onion is tender and spices are fragrant. Cool.

2 Place the chicken in batches in a food processor and process until just chopped. Do not overprocess.

3 Place the chicken, onion mixture, coriander and ½ teaspoon salt in a bowl, and mix together well. Using wetted hands, measure 1 tablespoon of mixture and shape into a ball. Repeat with the remaining mixture. Heat the remaining oil in a heavy-based frying pan, add the koftas in batches and cook for 4–5 minutes, or until well browned all over. Remove from the pan and cover.

4 Place the onion in a food processor or blender and process until smooth.

5 Heat the ghee in a frying pan. Add the onion and garlic, and cook, stirring, for 5 minutes, or until the onion juices evaporate and the mixture starts to thicken. Add the garam masala and turmeric, and cook for a further 2 minutes. Add the coconut milk, yoghurt, cream and ground almonds. Gently bring almost to the boil, then reduce the heat to medium and add the koftas. Cook, stirring occasionally, for 15 minutes, or until the koftas are cooked through. Stir in the coriander. Serve with steamed rice.

Cook chicken meatballs until well browned all over.

Place onion in a food processor or blender and process until smooth.

Cook onion until juices start to evaporate and mixture thickens.

Gaeng Phedyang Subarot (Thai Duck and Pineapple Curry)

PREPARATION TIME: 10 minutes
TOTAL COOKING TIME: 15 minutes
SERVES 4–6

1 tablespoon peanut oil
8 spring onions, sliced on the diagonal into
   3 cm lengths
2 cloves garlic, crushed
2–4 tablespoons red curry paste
750 g Chinese roast duck, chopped
400 ml coconut milk
450 g can pineapple pieces in syrup, drained
3 kaffir lime leaves
3 tablespoons chopped fresh coriander
2 tablespoons chopped fresh mint

1 Heat a wok until very hot, add the peanut oil and swirl to coat the side. Add the spring onion, garlic and red curry paste, and stir-fry for 1 minute, or until fragrant.

2 Add the roast duck pieces, coconut milk, drained pineapple pieces, kaffir lime leaves, and half the fresh coriander and mint. Bring to the boil, then reduce the heat and simmer for 10 minutes, or until the duck is heated through and the sauce has thickened slightly. Stir in the remaining fresh coriander and mint, and serve with jasmine rice.

Heat a wok until very hot, add the oil and swirl to coat.

Stir-fry the spring onion, garlic and curry paste until fragrant.

Simmer until duck is heated through and sauce has thickened.

Jamaican Curried Chicken

PREPARATION TIME: 30 minutes
TOTAL COOKING TIME: 1 hour
SERVES 6

60 g ghee or butter
2 tablespoons oil
1.5 kg chicken pieces
1 tablespoon coconut vinegar
500 g potatoes, cut into 4 cm cubes
2 large onions, sliced
2 small fresh red chillies, finely chopped
1 cinnamon stick
4 whole cloves
3 cups (750 ml) chicken stock
3 tablespoons plain flour
2½ tablespoons Indian curry powder
2 tablespoons dark brown sugar
½ teaspoon ground allspice (Jamaican pepper)
⅓ cup (80 ml) lime juice
400 ml coconut milk

Banana and pawpaw sambal
1½ tablespoons fresh lime juice
½ tablespoon Jamaican or dark rum
1 tablespoon dark brown sugar
1 tablespoon fresh coriander, finely chopped
¼–½ teaspoon Tabasco sauce
¼ teaspoon ground allspice (Jamaican pepper)
1½ firm bananas, peeled and sliced
½ small (250 g) pawpaw, peeled and diced
½ small red onion, finely chopped

1 Heat the ghee and oil in a large saucepan or casserole dish. Cook the chicken pieces in batches over medium heat for 10 minutes, or until browned.

2 Stir in the vinegar and allow to boil and evaporate. Add the potato, onion, chilli, cinnamon and cloves, and cook, stirring, for 3 minutes. Pour in chicken stock and bring to the boil.

3 Place the flour, curry powder, sugar and allspice in a small bowl. Pour in lime juice and stir to form a smooth paste. Stir the paste into the chicken mixture.

4 Reduce the heat, add the coconut milk to the pan and simmer, covered, for 30–40 minutes, or until the chicken and potato are tender and the sauce has slightly thickened.

5 To make the sambal, pour the lime juice and rum into a large bowl. Add the sugar, coriander, Tabasco sauce and allspice, and mix together well. Stir in the banana, pawpaw and onion.

6 Serve the curry with basmati rice and the banana and pawpaw sambal.

Murghabi Moolee (Duck and Coconut Curry)

PREPARATION TIME: 20 minutes
TOTAL COOKING TIME: 1 hour 15 minutes
SERVES 6

Curry paste
1 red onion, chopped
2 cloves garlic
2 coriander roots, chopped
2 teaspoons chopped fresh ginger
1½ teaspoons coriander seeds, dry-roasted
  and ground
1 teaspoon cardamom seeds, dry-roasted
  and ground
1 teaspoon fenugreek seeds, dry-roasted
  and ground
1 teaspoon brown mustard seeds, dry-
  roasted and ground
10 black peppercorns, ground
2 teaspoons garam masala
¼ teaspoon ground turmeric
2 teaspoons tamarind purée

6–8 duck breast fillets
1 red onion, sliced
½ cup (125 ml) white vinegar
2 cups (500 ml) coconut milk
2 tablespoons fresh coriander leaves

1 To make the curry paste, place all the ingredients in a blender and blend to a thick paste.

2 Trim any excess fat from the duck fillets, then place, skin-side-down, in a large saucepan and cook over medium heat for 10 minutes, or until the skin is brown and any remaining fat has melted. Turn the fillets over and cook for 5 minutes, or until tender. Remove and drain on paper towels.

3 Reserve 1 tablespoon duck fat, discard remaining fat. Add the onion and cook for 5 minutes, then add the curry paste and stir over low heat for 10 minutes, or until fragrant.

4 Return the duck to the pan and stir to coat with the paste. Stir in the vinegar, coconut milk, 1 teaspoon salt and ½ cup (125 ml) water. Simmer, covered, for 45 minutes, or until the fillets are tender. Stir in the coriander leaves just prior to serving. Serve with rice and naan bread.

Place curry paste ingredients in a blender and blend to a thick paste.

Use a sharp knife to trim excess fat from the duck breast fillets.

Gaeng Keo Wan Gai
(Thai Green Chicken Curry)

PREPARATION TIME: 40 minutes
TOTAL COOKING TIME: 30 minutes
SERVES 4–6

2 cups (500 ml) coconut cream, do not shake the can
4 tablespoons green curry paste
2 tablespoons grated palm sugar
2 tablespoons fish sauce
4 kaffir lime leaves, finely shredded
1 kg chicken thigh or breast fillets, cut into thick strips
200 g bamboo shoots, cut into thick strips
100 g snake beans, cut into 5 cm lengths
½ cup (15 g) fresh Thai basil leaves

1 Open the can of coconut cream and lift off the thick cream from the top, you should have about ½ cup (125 ml). Place the thick coconut cream in a wok or saucepan and bring to the boil. Add the curry paste, then reduce the heat and simmer for 15 minutes, or until fragrant and the oil starts to separate from the cream. Add the palm sugar, fish sauce and kaffir lime leaves to the pan.

2 Stir in the remaining coconut cream and the chicken, bamboo shoots and beans, and simmer for 15 minutes, or until the chicken is tender. Stir in the Thai basil and serve with rice.

Lift off the thick cream from the top of the can of coconut cream.

Simmer the coconut cream and curry paste until the oil separates.

Murgh Makhani (Butter Chicken)

PREPARATION TIME: 10 minutes
TOTAL COOKING TIME: 35 minutes
SERVES 4–6

2 tablespoons peanut oil
1 kg chicken thigh fillets, quartered
60 g butter or ghee
2 teaspoons garam masala
2 teaspoons sweet paprika
2 teaspoons ground coriander
1 tablespoon finely chopped fresh ginger
¼ teaspoon chilli powder
1 cinnamon stick
6 cardamom pods, bruised
350 g puréed tomatoes
1 tablespoon sugar
¼ cup (60 g) plain yoghurt
½ cup (125 ml) cream
1 tablespoon lemon juice

1 Heat a wok until very hot, add 1 tablespoon oil and swirl to coat. Add half the chicken thigh fillets and stir-fry for 4 minutes, or until browned. Remove. Add extra oil, as needed, and cook the remaining chicken. Remove.

2 Reduce the heat, add the butter to the wok and melt. Add the garam masala, sweet paprika, coriander, ginger, chilli powder, cinnamon stick and cardamom pods, and stir-fry for 1 minute, or until fragrant. Return the chicken to the wok and mix to coat in the spices.

3 Add the tomato and sugar, and simmer, stirring, for 15 minutes, or until the chicken is tender and the sauce has thickened.

4 Add the yoghurt, cream and juice and simmer for 5 minutes, or until the sauce has thickened slightly. Serve with rice and pappadums.

Stir-fry the chicken pieces in two batches until browned.

Simmer until chicken is tender and the sauce has thickened.

Vietnamese Mild Chicken Curry

PREPARATION TIME: 30 minutes
+ overnight refrigeration
TOTAL COOKING TIME: 1 hour 10 minutes
SERVES 6

4 large chicken Marylands
1 tablespoon good-quality Indian curry
  powder
1 teaspoon caster sugar
⅓ cup (80 ml) oil
500 g orange sweet potato, cut into 3 cm
  cubes
1 large onion, cut into thin wedges
4 cloves garlic, chopped
1 stem lemon grass, white part only, chopped
2 bay leaves
1 large carrot, cut into 1 cm pieces on the
  diagonal
400 ml coconut milk

1 Remove skin and any excess fat
from chicken. Pat dry with paper
towels and cut each piece into
3 even pieces, making 12 pieces.
Place the curry powder, sugar,

½ teaspoon black pepper and 2 teaspoons salt in a
bowl, and mix well. Rub curry mixture into chicken
pieces. Place the chicken pieces on a plate, cover
with plastic wrap and refrigerate overnight.

2 Heat oil in a large saucepan. Add sweet potato
and cook over medium heat for 3 minutes, or until
lightly golden. Remove with a slotted spoon.

3 Remove all but 2 tablespoons of the oil from pan.
Add the onion and cook, stirring, for 5 minutes.
Then add the garlic, lemon grass and bay leaves,
and cook for 2 minutes.

4 Add chicken and cook, stirring, over medium heat
for 5 minutes, or until well coated in the mixture
and starting to change colour. Add 1 cup (250 ml)
water and simmer, covered, for 20 minutes. Stir
once or twice.

5 Stir in the carrot, sweet potato and coconut milk,
and simmer, uncovered, stirring occasionally, for
30 minutes, or until the chicken is cooked and
tender. Be careful not to break up the sweet
potato cubes. Serve with steamed rice.

*Remove the skin and any excess
fat from the chicken.*

*Cut each chicken Maryland into
three even pieces.*

*Rub the spice mixture into each
of the chicken pieces.*

Whole Fish in Malaysian Sauce

PREPARATION TIME: 35 minutes
+ 10 minutes soaking
TOTAL COOKING TIME: 1 hour 10 minutes
SERVES 6

Curry paste
12 dried chillies
5 cloves garlic, sliced
2 red onions, chopped
2 stems lemon grass, white part only, sliced
2 x 1.5 cm piece fresh turmeric, sliced
2 teaspoons shrimp powder, dry-roasted
2 tablespoons ground almonds
2 teaspoons grated fresh galangal
¼ cup (60 ml) oil

2 x 800 g–1 kg whole snapper, gutted and scaled
½ cup (155 g) tamarind purée
1 teaspoon palm sugar
2 tablespoons fish sauce
1 cup (250 ml) coconut cream
fresh Vietnamese mint leaves, to garnish

1 To make the curry paste, soak the chillies in 1 cup (250 ml) boiling water for 10 minutes, drain and place in a blender with the remaining curry paste ingredients. Blend to a thick paste.

2 Preheat the oven to moderate 180°C (350°F/Gas 4). Wash fish and score in the thickest part. Pat dry with paper towels and place in an ovenproof dish.

3 Heat a wok over medium heat, add the curry paste and cook for 10 minutes, or until fragrant. Add the tamarind purée and ½ cup (125 ml) water, and cook for 5 minutes. Then add an extra 1½ cups (375 ml) water and bring to the boil. Reduce the heat and simmer for 10 minutes.

4 Stir in the palm sugar, fish sauce and coconut cream, and simmer for a further 5 minutes, or until heated through and thickened.

5 Pour the sauce over the fish and cover with foil. Cook in the oven for 35–40 minutes, or until cooked through. Garnish with the mint and serve with rice and steamed greens.

Blend curry paste ingredients in a blender to a thick paste.

Score fish in the thickest part to ensure even cooking.

Simmer the sauce until heated through and thickened.

Crab Curry

PREPARATION TIME: 25 minutes
TOTAL COOKING TIME: 20 minutes
SERVES 6

4 raw large blue swimmer or mud crabs
1 tablespoon oil
1 large onion, finely chopped
2 cloves garlic, crushed
1 stem lemon grass, white part only, finely
  chopped
1 teaspoon sambal oelek
1 teaspoon ground cumin
1 teaspoon ground turmeric
1 teaspoon ground coriander
270 ml coconut cream
2 cups (500 ml) chicken stock
⅓ cup (20 g) firmly packed fresh basil leaves

1 Pull back the apron and remove the top shell from the crabs. Remove the intestines and grey feathery gills. Cut each crab into four pieces. Use a cracker to crack the claws open; this will make it easier to eat later and will also allow the flavours to get into the crab meat.

2 Heat the oil in large saucepan or wok. Add the onion, garlic, lemon grass and sambal oelek, and cook for 2–3 minutes, or until softened.

3 Add the cumin, turmeric, coriander and ½ teaspoon salt, and cook for a further 2 minutes, or until fragrant.

4 Stir in the coconut cream and stock. Bring to the boil, then reduce the heat, add the crab pieces and cook, stirring occasionally, for 10 minutes, or until the liquid has reduced and thickened slightly and the crabs are cooked through. Stir in the basil and serve with steamed rice.

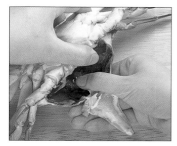

Pull back the apron and remove the top shell from the crab.

Remove the intestines and grey feathery gills from the crabs.

Crack claws to allow flavours to penetrate while cooking.

Masala Jheengari (Spicy Prawns)

PREPARATION TIME: 30 minutes
+ 15 minutes standing
TOTAL COOKING TIME: 55 minutes
SERVES 4–6

1 kg raw medium prawns, shelled, deveined, tails intact (reserve shells and heads)
1 teaspoon ground turmeric
¼ cup (60 ml) oil
2 onions, finely chopped
4–6 cloves garlic, finely chopped
1–2 small green chillies, seeded and chopped
2 teaspoons ground cumin
2 teaspoons ground coriander
1 teaspoon paprika
⅓ cup (90 g) plain yoghurt
⅓ cup (80 ml) thick cream
4 tablespoons chopped fresh coriander leaves

1 Bring 1 litre water to the boil in a large saucepan. Add the reserved prawn shells and heads, and reduce the heat and simmer for 2 minutes. Skim any scum that forms on the surface during cooking with a skimmer or slotted spoon. Drain, discard the shells and heads and return the liquid to the pan. You will need 3 cups (750 ml) liquid. Make up with water, if necessary. Add the turmeric and peeled prawns, and cook for 1 minute, or until the prawns just turn pink. Remove the prawns.

2 Heat the oil in a large saucepan. Add the onion and cook, stirring, for 8 minutes, or until lightly golden brown. Take care not to burn the onion. Add the garlic and chilli, and cook for 2 minutes, then add the cumin, coriander and paprika, and cook, stirring, for 2–3 minutes, or until fragrant.

3 Gradually add the reserved stock, bring to the boil and cook, stirring occasionally, for 35 minutes, or until the mixture has reduced by half and thickened.

4 Remove from the heat and stir in yoghurt. Add the prawns and stir over low heat for 2–3 minutes, or until the prawns are warmed through. Do not boil. Stir in the cream and coriander leaves. Cover and leave to stand for 15 minutes to allow the flavours to infuse. Reheat gently and serve with rice.

Skim any scum on the surface with a skimmer or slotted spoon.

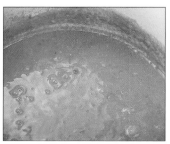

Boil the mixture until it has reduced by half and thickened.

Fish Ball Curry

PREPARATION TIME: 20 minutes
TOTAL COOKING TIME: 25 minutes
SERVES 6

1 large onion, chopped
1 teaspoon sambal oelek
1 tablespoon finely chopped fresh ginger
1 stem lemon grass, white part only, finely
   chopped
3 tablespoons fresh chopped coriander
   roots
½ teaspoon ground cardamom
1 tablespoon tomato paste
1 tablespoon oil
1 tablespoon fish sauce
2 cups (500 ml) coconut milk
750 g fish balls (if frozen, thawed)
3 tablespoons chopped fresh coriander
fresh coriander, extra, to garnish

1 Put the onion, sambal oelek, ginger, lemon grass, coriander, cardamom and tomato paste in a food processor, and process to a smooth paste.

2 Heat the oil in a large saucepan. Add the spice paste and cook, stirring, over medium heat for 4 minutes, or until fragrant.

3 Stir in the fish sauce, coconut milk and 2 cups (500 ml) water. Bring to the boil, then reduce the heat and simmer for 15 minutes, or until the sauce has reduced and thickened slightly.

4 Add the fish balls and cook for 2 minutes. Do not to overcook or the fish balls will be tough and rubbery. Stir in the coriander and garnish with extra coriander. Serve with rice.

Process the ingredients for the curry paste to a smooth paste.

Reduce the heat and simmer until reduced and slightly thickened.

Goan Machchi (Goan Fish Curry)

PREPARATION TIME: 20 minutes
TOTAL COOKING TIME: 35 minutes
SERVES 6

¼ cup (60 ml) oil
1 large onion, finely chopped
4–5 cloves garlic, chopped
2 teaspoons grated fresh ginger
4–6 small dried red chillies
1 tablespoon coriander seeds
2 teaspoons cumin seeds
1 teaspoon ground turmeric
¼ teaspoon chilli powder
⅓ cup (30 g) desiccated coconut
270 ml coconut milk
2 tomatoes, peeled and chopped
2 tablespoons tamarind purée
1 tablespoon white vinegar
6 curry leaves
1 kg boneless, skinless firm fish fillets, such
  as flake or ling, cut into 8 cm pieces

1 Heat the oil in a large saucepan. Add the onion and cook, stirring, over low heat for 10 minutes, or until softened and lightly golden. Add the garlic and ginger, and cook for a further 2 minutes.

2 Meanwhile, place the dried chillies, spices and desiccated coconut in a frying pan, and dry-fry, stirring constantly, over medium heat for 2 minutes, or until aromatic. Place in a spice grinder and finely grind.

3 Add the spice mixture, coconut milk, tomato, tamarind, vinegar and curry leaves to the onion mixture. Stir to mix thoroughly, add 1 cup (250 ml) water and simmer for 10 minutes, or until the tomato has softened and the mixture has thickened slightly. Stir frequently.

4 Add the fish and cook, covered, over low heat for 10 minutes, or until cooked through. Stir gently once or twice during cooking and add a little water if the mixture is too thick. Serve immediately with rice and pappadums.

Dry-fry dried chillies, spices and desiccated coconut until fragrant.

Place the dry-fried spices in a spice grinder and finely grind.

Simmer until tomato has softened and mixture has thickened .

Western Prawn Curry

PREPARATION TIME: 25 minutes
TOTAL COOKING TIME: 15 minutes
SERVES 4–6

50 g butter
1 onion, finely chopped
1 clove garlic, crushed
1½ tablespoons curry powder
2 tablespoons plain flour
2 cups (500 ml) milk
1 kg raw medium prawns, peeled and
  deveined
1½ tablespoons lemon juice
2 teaspoons sherry, optional
1 tablespoon finely chopped fresh parsley

1 Heat the butter in a large saucepan. Add the onion and garlic, and cook for 5 minutes, or until softened. Add the curry powder and cook for 1 minute, then stir in the flour and cook for a further 1 minute.

2 Remove from the heat and stir in the milk until smooth. Return to the heat and stir constantly until the sauce has thickened. Simmer for 2 minutes and then stir in the prawns. Continue to simmer for 5 minutes, or until the prawns are just cooked.

3 Stir in the lemon juice, sherry and parsley and serve immediately with rice.

Add the garlic and onion to the butter, and cook until softened.

Return saucepan to the heat and stir mixture until thickened.

Add the prawns and continue to simmer until just cooked.

65

Kaeng Massaman (Thai Musaman Vegetable Curry)

PREPARATION TIME: 25 minutes
TOTAL COOKING TIME: 45 minutes
SERVES 4–6

Curry paste
1 tablespoon oil
1 teaspoon coriander seeds
1 teaspoon cumin seeds
8 cloves
½ teaspoon fennel seeds
seeds from 4 cardamom pods
6 red Asian shallots, chopped
3 cloves garlic, chopped
1 teaspoon finely chopped lemon grass,
  white part only
1 teaspoon finely chopped fresh galangal
4 large dried red chillies
1 teaspoon ground nutmeg
1 teaspoon white pepper

1 tablespoon oil
250 g pickling onions
500 g small new potatoes
300 g carrots, cut into 3 cm pieces
225 g can whole champignons, drained
1 cinnamon stick
1 kaffir lime leaf
1 bay leaf
1 cup (250 ml) coconut cream
1 tablespoon lime juice
3 teaspoons grated palm sugar
1 tablespoon shredded fresh Thai basil
  leaves
1 tablespoon crushed roasted peanuts
fresh Thai basil leaves, extra, to garnish

1 To make the curry paste, heat the oil in a frying pan over low heat, add the coriander, cumin, cloves, fennel seeds and cardamom seeds, and cook for 1–2 minutes, or until fragrant. Place in a food processor and add the shallots, garlic, lemon grass, galangal, chillies, nutmeg and white pepper. Process until smooth, adding a little water as necessary.

2 Heat the oil in a large saucepan, add the curry paste and cook, stirring, over medium heat for 2 minutes, or until fragrant. Add the vegetables, cinnamon stick, kaffir lime leaf, bay leaf, salt to taste and enough water to cover (about 2 cups (500 ml)), and bring to the boil. Reduce the heat and simmer, covered, stirring, for 30–35 minutes, or until the vegetables are cooked. Stir in the coconut cream and cook, uncovered, for 4 minutes, stirring frequently, until thickened slightly. Stir in the lime juice, palm sugar and shredded Thai basil. Add a little water if the sauce is too dry. Garnish with the peanuts and Thai basil leaves.

Chu Chee Tofu (Tofu in a Light Thai Red Curry)

PREPARATION TIME: 20 minutes
TOTAL COOKING TIME: 20 minutes
SERVES 6

Curry paste
10 small red chillies
50 g red Asian shallots, peeled
1 tablespoon finely chopped fresh coriander stem and root
1 stem lemon grass, white part only, chopped
2 tablespoons grated fresh galangal
2 cloves garlic
1 tablespoon ground coriander
1 teaspoon ground cumin
1 teaspoon black peppercorns
½ teaspoon ground turmeric
1 tablespoon lime juice

1 tablespoon oil
1 onion, finely chopped
2 cups (500 ml) coconut milk
200 g fried tofu puffs, halved on the diagonal
fresh coriander sprigs, to garnish

1 To make the curry paste, place all the ingredients in a food processor or spice grinder and process until smooth.

2 Heat the oil in a large saucepan, add the onion and cook over medium heat for 4–5 minutes, or until starting to brown. Add 3 tablespoons of the curry paste and cook, stirring, for 2 minutes.

3 Stir in the coconut milk and ½ cup (125 ml) water, and season with salt. Bring slowly to the boil, stirring constantly. Add the tofu puffs, then reduce the heat and simmer, stirring frequently, for 5 minutes, or until the sauce thickens slightly. Garnish with the fresh coriander sprigs.

Grind all the ingredients for the curry paste until smooth.

Cook the onions over medium heat until just starting to brown.

Add the tofu and simmer until the sauce has thickened slightly.

Dum Alu (Smothered Potatoes)

PREPARATION TIME: 20 minutes

TOTAL COOKING TIME: 30 minutes

SERVES 6

Curry paste
4 cardamom pods
1 teaspoon grated fresh ginger
2 cloves garlic
6 small red chillies
1 teaspoon cumin seeds
¼ cup (40 g) raw cashew nut pieces
1 tablespoon white poppy seeds (khus)
1 cinnamon stick
6 cloves

1 kg potatoes, cubed
2 onions, roughly chopped
2 tablespoons oil
½ teaspoon ground turmeric
1 teaspoon besan (chickpea flour)
1 cup (250 g) plain yoghurt
fresh coriander leaves, to garnish

1 To make the curry paste, lightly crush cardamom pods with the flat side of a heavy knife. Remove the seeds, discarding the pods. Place the seeds and the remaining curry paste ingredients in a food processor, and process to a smooth paste.

2 Bring a large saucepan of lightly salted water to the boil. Add the potato and cook for 5–6 minutes, or until just tender. Drain.

3 Place the onions in a food processor and process in short bursts until it is finely ground but not puréed. Heat the oil in a large saucepan, add the ground onion and cook over low heat for 5 minutes. Add the curry paste and cook, stirring, for a further 5 minutes, or until fragrant. Stir in the potato, turmeric, salt to taste and 1 cup (250 ml) water.

4 Reduce the heat and simmer, tightly covered, for 10 minutes, or until the potato is cooked but not breaking up and the sauce has thickened slightly.

5 Combine the chickpea flour with the yoghurt, add to the potato mixture and cook, stirring, over low heat for 5 minutes, or until thickened again. Garnish with the coriander leaves.

Add the curry paste to the onion and cook until fragrant.

Simmer until the potato is cooked but not breaking up.

Balti Okra

PREPARATION TIME: 15 minutes
TOTAL COOKING TIME: 45 minutes
SERVES 6

750 g okra
⅓ cup (80 ml) oil
1 onion, finely chopped
1 teaspoon chilli powder
½ teaspoon ground turmeric
2 tomatoes, quartered
1 tablespoon garam masala
¼ teaspoon ground cardamom seeds
pinch grated nutmeg

1 Remove the stems and cut the okra into 2.5 cm lengths.

2 Heat the oil in a frying pan, add the onion and cook for 10 minutes, or until golden. Add the okra, chilli powder, turmeric, tomato, and salt to taste, and cook, covered, stirring frequently, for 30–35 minutes, or until the okra is tender. Add a little water, if required. Add the garam masala, ground cardamom and nutmeg, and cook, stirring, for 1–2 minutes.

Remove the okra stems and cut into short lengths.

Heat the oil, add onion and cook for 10 minutes, or until golden.

Add okra, chilli powder, turmeric, tomato and salt; cook until tender.

Channa Masala (Chickpea Curry)

PREPARATION TIME: 10 minutes
+ overnight soaking
TOTAL COOKING TIME: 1 hour 15 minutes
SERVES 6

1 cup (220 g) dried chickpeas
2 tablespoons oil
2 onions, finely chopped
2 large ripe tomatoes, chopped
½ teaspoon ground coriander
1 teaspoon ground cumin
1 teaspoon chilli powder
¼ teaspoon ground turmeric
1 tablespoon channa (chole) masala
20 g ghee or butter
1 small white onion, sliced
fresh mint and coriander leaves, to garnish

1 Place the chickpeas in a bowl, cover with water and leave to soak overnight. Drain, rinse and place in a large saucepan. Cover with plenty of water and bring to the boil, then reduce the heat and simmer for 40 minutes, or until soft. Drain.

2 Heat the oil in a large saucepan, add the onion and cook over medium heat for 15 minutes, or until golden brown. Add the tomato, ground coriander and cumin, chilli powder, turmeric and channa (chole) masala, and 2 cups (500 ml) water, and cook for 10 minutes, or until the tomato is soft. Add the chickpeas, season well with salt and cook for 7–10 minutes, or until the sauce thickens. Transfer to a serving dish. Place the ghee or butter on top and allow to melt before serving. Garnish with sliced onion and fresh mint and coriander leaves.

Cook the onion in a large saucepan until golden brown.

Add the chickpeas and cook until the sauce thickens.

Pancharatna Dhal (Five Jewel Lentil Curry)

PREPARATION TIME: 15 minutes
+ overnight soaking +2 hours soaking
TOTAL COOKING TIME: 1 hour 10 minutes
SERVES 6

¼ cup (55 g) red kidney beans
¼ cup (50 g) black-eyed beans
¼ cup (60 g) red lentils
¼ cup (55 g) split yellow peas
¼ cup (55 g) mung dhal (split mung beans)
¼ teaspoon ground turmeric
2 tablespoons oil
1 teaspoon mustard seeds
1 teaspoon cumin seeds
4 red chillies, chopped coarsely
¼ teaspoon asafoetida
5 curry leaves
1 onion, sliced
3 cloves garlic
1 teaspoon ground cumin
1 teaspoon ground coriander
¼ cup (60 ml) lemon juice
fresh coriander leaves, to garnish

1 Soak the kidney beans and black-eyed beans in cold water separately overnight. Drain and rinse thoroughly. Add to a medium saucepan, cover with fresh water and cook over medium heat for 45 minutes, or until softened.

2 Combine red lentils, yellow split peas and mung dhal, cover with water and soak for 2 hours. Rinse thoroughly. Place in a saucepan, cover with fresh water, add turmeric and salt to taste, and cook over medium heat for 30 minutes, or until tender.

3 Heat the oil in a large saucepan over medium heat and add mustard seeds. When seeds start to pop, add cumin seeds, chilli, asafoetida and curry leaves. Cook for 1 minute, then add onion and garlic. Cook over low heat for 8 minutes, or the onion is golden.

4 Add lentils, peas, beans, cumin and coriander to the onion. Cook over medium heat for 5–10 minutes, or until beans are tender. Remove from heat, stir in lemon juice and garnish with coriander leaves.

Wear gloves when chopping the chillies.

Cook red lentils, split peas and mung dhal until softened.

Add the onion to the pan and cook until golden brown.

Bhajia Kari (Onion Fritters in Curry Sauce)

PREPARATION TIME: 20 minutes
TOTAL COOKING TIME: 30 minutes
SERVES 4

Bhajias
1 cup (125 g) besan (chickpea flour)
¼ teaspoon ground turmeric
½ teaspoon chilli powder
¼ teaspoon asafoetida
1 onion, thinly sliced
oil, for deep-frying

2 tablespoons oil
1 teaspoon grated fresh ginger
2 cloves garlic, crushed
425 g can crushed tomatoes
¼ teaspoon ground turmeric
½ teaspoon chilli powder
1½ teaspoons ground cumin
1 teaspoon ground coriander
1½ tablespoons garam masala
1 cup (250 ml) cream
chopped fresh coriander leaves, to garnish

1 To make the bhajias, combine the besan, turmeric, chilli powder and asafoetida with ½ cup (125 ml) water, and salt to taste. Whisk to make a smooth batter, then stir in the onion.

2 Fill a deep heavy-based saucepan one-third full of oil and heat to 160°C (315°F), or until a cube of bread dropped into the oil browns in 30 seconds. Add spoonfuls of the onion mixture in batches and cook for 1–2 minutes, or until golden brown all over. Drain.

3 Heat the oil in a frying pan, add the ginger and garlic, and cook for 2 minutes, or until fragrant. Add the tomato, turmeric, chilli powder, cumin, coriander, salt to taste and 1 cup (250 ml) water. Bring to the boil, then reduce the heat and simmer for 5 minutes, or until thickened slightly. Add the garam masala, stir in the cream and simmer for 1–2 minutes. Remove from heat, pour over the bhajias and garnish with the coriander leaves. Serve immediately.

Whisk the batter ingredients together until smooth.

Cook spoonfuls of mixture in batches until golden brown.

Bring to the boil, reduce heat and simmer until thickened slightly.

All our recipes are thoroughly tested in a specially developed test kitchen. Standard metric measuring cups and spoons are used in the development of our recipes. All cup and spoon measurements are level. We have used 60 g (2 1/4 oz/Grade 3) eggs in all recipes. Sizes of cans vary from manufacturer to manufacturer and between countries – use the can size closest to the one suggested in the recipe.

CONVERSION GUIDE

1 cup = 250 ml (9 fl oz)
1 teaspoon = 5 ml
1 Australian tablespoon = 20 ml (4 teaspoons)
1 UK/US tablespoon = 15 ml (3 teaspoons)

Where temperature ranges are indicated, the lower figure applies to gas ovens, the higher to electric ovens. This allows for the fact that the flame in gas ovens generates a drier heat, which effectively cooks food faster than the moister heat of an electric oven, even if the temperature setting is the same.

DRY MEASURES	LIQUID MEASURES	LINEAR MEASURES
30 g = 1 oz	30 ml = 1 fl oz	6 mm = 1/4 inch
250 g = 9 oz	125 ml = 4 fl oz	1 cm = 1/2 inch
500 g = 1 lb 2 oz	250 ml = 9 fl oz	2.5 cm = 1 inch

	°C	°F	Gas mark
Very slow	120	250	1/2
Slow	150	300	2
Mod slow	160	325	3
Moderate	180	350	4
Mod hot	190(g)–210(e)	375–425	5
Hot	200(g)–240(e)	400–475	6
Very hot	230(g)–260(e)	450–525	8

(g) = gas (e) = electric
Note: For fan-forced ovens, check your appliance manual, but as a general rule, set the oven temperature to 20°C lower than the temperature indicated in the recipe.

CUP CONVERSIONS – DRY INGREDIENTS

1 cup almonds, slivered whole = 125 g (4 1/2 oz)
1 cup cheese, lightly packed processed cheddar
   = 155 g (5 1/2 oz)
1 cup wheat flour = 125 g (4 1/2 oz)
1 cup wholemeal flour = 140 g (5 oz)
1 cup minced (ground) meat = 250 g (9 oz)
1 cup pasta shapes = 125 g (4 1/2 oz)
1 cup raisins = 170 g (6 oz)
1 cup rice, short grain, raw = 200 g (7 oz)
1 cup sesame seeds = 160 g (6 oz)
1 cup split peas = 250 g (9 oz)

INTERNATIONAL GLOSSARY

capsicum	sweet bell pepper	cornflour	cornstarch
chick pea	garbanzo bean	eggplant	aubergine
chilli	chile, chili pepper	spring onion	scallion
		zucchini	courgette

Published in 2010 by Bay Books, an imprint of Murdoch Books Pty Limited
This edition published 2010 for Index Books Ltd

Murdoch Books Australia
Pier 8/9, 23 Hickson Road
Millers Point NSW 2000
Phone: +61 (0) 2 8220 2000
Fax: +61 (0) 2 8220 2558
www.murdochbooks.com.au

Murdoch Books UK Limited
Erico House, 6th Floor
93–99 Upper Richmond Road
Putney, London SW15 2TG
Phone: +44 (0) 20 8785 5995
Fax: +44 (0) 20 8785 5985
www.murdochbooks.co.uk

ISBN: 978-1-74196-974-0

PRINTED IN CHINA.

IMPORTANT: Those who might be at risk from the effects of salmonella poisoning (the elderly, pregnant women, young children and those suffering from immune deficiency diseases) should consult their doctor with any concerns about eating raw eggs.

OVEN GUIDE: You may find cooking times vary depending on the oven you are using. For fan-forced ovens, as a general rule, set the oven temperature to 20°C (35°F) lower than indicated in the recipe.